GUIDE TO THE PAPHOS MOSAICS

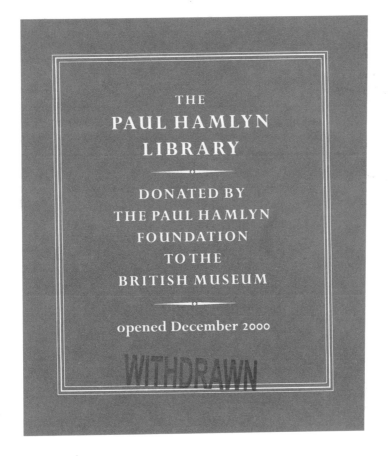

GUIDE TO THE PAPHOS MOSAICS

Text by
W.A. Daszewski
D. Michaelides

SERIES OF GUIDE-BOOKS
PUBLISHED BY THE BANK OF CYPRUS CULTURAL FOUNDATION
IN COLLABORATION WITH
THE DEPARTMENT OF ANTIQUITIES

ISBN 9963-42-010-9

CONTENTS

Front Cover

Silenus with panthers, detail from the Triumph of Dionysos;
House of Dionysos.

Credits

Series Editor: *Maria Iacovou.*
Ground Plans: *Department of Antiquities.*
Mosaic Photographs: *Andreas Malecos (House of Dionysos);*
                    Department of Antiquities (Houses
                    of Orpheus and Theseus);
                    Polish Archaeological Mission
                    (House of Aion).
Colour Separation: *D. Hadjistillis, G. Voulgarides, Greece;*
                  Leogravure, Beirut;
                  Grawo Ltd., Nicosia.
Book Design: *Maria Iacovou.*
Printing: *Chr. Nicolaou, Nicosia.*

PREFACE

In 1987 the Bank of Cyprus Cultural Foundation launched a major publication project for the production of a series of richly illustrated guide-books to the ancient monuments and archaeological sites of Cyprus. The goal is to issue one guide *per annum* in four languages. The text is provided by the Department of Antiquities and it is based on the official reports of scholars currently active in the field of Cypriot archaeology. The purpose of this long-term and ambitious project is dual: on the one hand, it supports and promotes cultural tourism; on the other, it offers a substantial financial support to the Department of Antiquities, since net proceeds from the sale of the books are deposited in a special fund for the restoration of ancient monuments.

After the tragic events of 1974 which resulted in the occupation by the Turkish Army of that part of Cyprus which includes Famagusta and Kyrenia, Kato Paphos, known in antiquity as Nea Paphos, has grown into an important tourist centre. Once the capital of Graeco-Roman Cyprus, Nea Paphos has been included in the World Heritage List of UNESCO.

The text of the *Guide to the Paphos Mosaics* was written by Dr. W.A. Daszewski and Dr. D. Michaelides. Both scholars are directors of excavations at Nea Paphos and specialists in the study of mosaics. Ground plans and photographs for the Houses of Orpheus, Theseus and Aion were provided by the Department of Antiquities. The new photographs for the mosaics of the House of Dionysos were taken by Andreas Malecos and belong to the photographic archive of the Cultural Foundation.

We expect that with the continuing collaboration of the Department of Antiquities and the unfailing interest of its Director, the guide-book series of our Cultural Foundation will make a contribution to the preservation and presentation of our island's heritage.

Andreas Patsalides
Chairman
Bank of Cyprus
Cultural Foundation

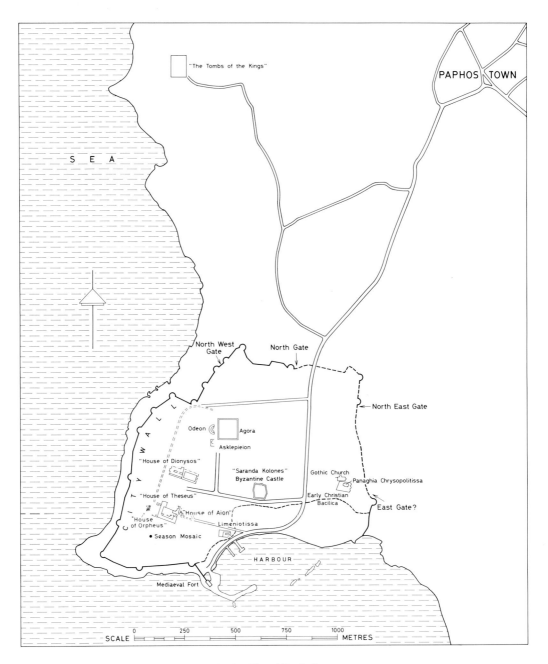

"The Tombs of the Kings"

PAPHOS TOWN

S E A

North West Gate

North Gate

North East Gate

Odeon

Agora

Asklepieion

"House of Dionysos"

"Saranda Kolones"
Byzantine Castle

Gothic Church

Panaghia Chrysopolitissa

CITY WALL

"House of Theseus"

Early Christian
Bacilica

East Gate?

"House
of Orpheus"

"House of Aion"

Limeniotissa

● Season Mosaic

HARBOUR

Mediaeval Fort

| SCALE | 0 | 250 | 500 | 750 | 1000 | METRES |

Fig. 1. Plan of Nea Paphos.

A BRIEF HISTORY OF NEA PAPHOS

Although Nea Paphos was destined to play one of the most important roles in the history of Cyprus, relatively little is known about its early days. Strabo (late 1st cent. B.C.) and Pausanias (2nd cent. A.D.) preserve a tradition according to which the city was founded in the 12th cent. B.C., after the end of the Trojan War, by Agapenor king of Tegea (Greece). Nowadays, however, this legend is taken to refer not to Nea Paphos but to Palaepaphos (modern Kouklia) which was then a prosperous town and had a world famous sanctuary dedicated to Aphrodite. Nea Paphos instead, appears to have been founded much later, towards the close of the 4th cent. B.C., by Nicocles, the last king of Palaepaphos.

Nea Paphos is situated on a small promontory on the SW coast of the island, and occupies a site on which (according to recent archaeological evidence) there was an earlier settlement that had grown around a small, sheltered bay − the future harbour of Nea Paphos. The town occupies an area of about 950.000 square metres, the whole of which is girt by high walls (Fig. 1). Part of the ancient street system has been investigated in the south-western sector of the town (see below, Villa of Theseus). This shows that right from the beginning, the town was built on an orthogonal plan based on a grid of streets cutting each other at right angles and forming rectangular *insulae* (blocks of buildings). Within this street system, which appears to have remained in use (with only minor changes) throughout the history of the town, there were well defined areas of commercial (near the Odeion) and residential (west of the harbour) character.

Soon after the late 4th cent. B.C. when Nea Paphos was founded, Cyprus became part of the kingdom of the Ptolemies, the Graeco-Macedonian rulers of Egypt, who had their capital at Alexandria. The Ptolemies placed special importance on Nea Paphos for a variety of reasons. Of these, the most important was its proximity to Alexandria and its good harbour which was the most important military outpost of the Ptolemies outside Egypt. Nea Paphos was also situated near the hills that provided the vast quantities of timber necessary to the Ptolemies for ship building. Most of the timber must have gone to Egypt; there is, however, evidence which indicates that very large ships were being built in Paphos itself from local timber. The town served as the centre of Ptolemaic administration on the island (see below, clay sealings from Room 6 of the House of Dionysos) and soon became the political and economic centre of the district. Such was its importance that by the 2nd cent. B.C. the Ptolemies made it the capital of the whole of Cyprus. Here resided the *strategos*, the supreme military commander who governed the island in the name of the Ptolemaic kings − who themselves often resided at Nea Paphos. The town was also one of a small number of centres on the island that enjoyed the right to mint coins (see below, the Ptolemaic coin hoard in Room 13 of the House of Dionysos).

In 58 B.C. Cyprus was annexed by Rome. Paphos remained the capital and continued to be the centre of all political and administrative life on the island. It was the only Cypriot town that retained the right to mint coins, and it was here, of course, that the Roman proconsul resided. As the town grew in importance it accumulated a number of titles, such as Augusta and Claudia Flavia Paphos, which reflect the favours conferred upon her by various Roman Emperors. These reached their peak by the Severan period when Nea Paphos was named "Sebaste Claudia Flavia, the sacred metropolis of all the towns in Cyprus". It is, in fact, during the Antonine and Severan periods (second half of 2nd / early 3rd cent. A.D.) that Nea Paphos appears to have reached the highest point of its importance and prosperity. This is reflected by the number of buildings, both public and private, which survive from this period, and the opulence of their decoration. The tombs of this period too, show an unusual variety and wealth of grave goods.

Of the public buildings so far investigated or attested in Paphos, mention can be made of an Agora, a Theatre, an Amphitheatre, an Odeion and an Asklepieion. There were also temples dedicated to Aphrodite, Artemis, Apollo, Zeus, Leto and probably Dionysos, as well as cult centres for the worship of rulers — first the Ptolemaic kings and later the Roman emperors. By contrast, although, as recorded in the Acts of the Apostles, Christianity was introduced to Nea Paphos as early as the mid 1st cent. A.D. by Sts Paul and Barnabas, there are no known Christian cult centres that can be dated to before the 4th cent. A.D.

Nea Paphos was severely damaged by earthquakes on several occasions, most notably in the late 1st cent. B.C. and the second half of the 1st cent. A.D. A series of violent tremors during the first half of the 4th cent. A.D., however, was especially devastating and badly ruined most Cypriot cities including Nea Paphos. In the rebuilding that followed, political, strategic and other reasons dictated that

precedence was given to Salamis. It was renamed Constantia and soon became the capital of the island. Life in Paphos did not cease, however, and by the end of the 4th cent. A.D. many buildings were rebuilt and richly decorated. All the same, Nea Paphos never regained her metropolitan status, even though it became the see of a bishop (first attested at the first Ecumenical Council of Nicaea in A.D. 325). Several splendid churches were erected in Paphos during this period, including the Early Christian Basilica of Chrysopolitissa, one of the largest buildings known on the island.

The mid 7th cent. A.D. saw the beginning of a series of Arab raids that led Cyprus into one of the darkest periods of her history. From this point on, Paphos suffered a slow but steady decline. The town was much reduced in size and nothing of importance appears to have been built for several centuries. Nea Paphos was to regain some of her importance in later times. First, during the period following A.D. 965 when the island once more came to form part of the Byzantine Empire; and later, under Frankish rule, when the Lusignan kings reigned over Cyprus (A.D. 1192 - 1489). During this period Paphos was adorned with several Gothic churches and castles were built for her defense (the castle of Saranda Colones and the castle by the harbour).

The decline, however, set in once more towards the end of the Lusignan period. It continued during the Venetian period (A.D. 1489-1570) and worsened under the Ottoman Turks that were to rule the island for about 300 years. The population had gradually began to move further inland to the safer and healthier plateau where the present town of Paphos (Ktima) now stands. Meanwhile, Nea Paphos continued to diminish in size. Part of its harbour silted up and the area around it was taken over by marshes. In fact, the only things that bring Paphos out of almost total oblivion during this period are the chronicles of pilgrims that visited it on their way to the Holy Land.

These contrast the miserable houses of their days to the splendid ruins of the past, and almost invariably complain of the unhealthy air of the place − something to be attributed probably to the marshes around the harbour.

D.M.

THE HOUSE OF DIONYSOS

The Discovery

A chance discovery made more than 25 years ago, has brought to light what still remains the most spectacular group of mosaics in Cyprus. During levelling operations in 1962, at the locality *Ktiston,* a large number of mosaic fragments and tesserae were found. This led the Department of Antiquities to halt all activity in the area and to carry out first a trial and then a systematic excavation of the site. This was done under the direction of the late K. Nicolaou of the Department of Antiquities and most of the work was completed between 1962 and 1965.

The excavations brought to light a large and wealthy residence of the Roman period, the first of its type to be found in Paphos and in Cyprus as a whole. The size of the building and the wealth of its mosaic decoration led to an initial identification of the owner with some high Roman official or even with the Proconsul himself. This identification, however, can now be dismissed for several reasons: the probable Proconsul's residence (known as the Villa of Theseus) has since been discovered and excavated. Moreover, as more and more

mosaic floors are located in the surrounding area, it is becoming clear that such rich decoration was not the exception but the norm for Paphos during the mid-Roman period. So, as far as the House of Dionysos is concerned, all that can be said with certainty is that it was one of several wealthy houses in one of the best quarters of ancient Paphos (Fig. 1).

The building occupies an area of about 2000 square metres, of which 556 are covered with mosaic floors. As Dionysos (Bacchus), the god of wine, features rather prominently in some of these mosaics, the building has been named the House of Dionysos.

The Building
(all room numbers refer to the plan on Fig. 3).

After the completion of the excavation the Department of Antiquities erected a roof over the mosaics to protect them from rain and direct sunlight. This roof was destroyed during the bombing of the area by Turkish airplanes in 1974. The present, more efficient shed was constructed in 1977. It only covers the area with mosaic floors, and although the rest of the building is not open to the public, some words on the house as a whole are necessary.

The mosaics (except the one now exhibited in Room 1) belong to the last of a series of buildings that once stood on this spot. Excavations carried out in some areas under the mosaics show that this last building made use of foundations and walls of an earlier building datable to the Flavian period, which itself stood on a series of earlier structures. The earliest of these appears to have been a sanctuary cut into the bedrock. A unique bone knife handle on which the god Harpokrates is depicted (Fig. 2) was found in this sanctuary. It is exhibited in the Paphos District Museum and shows the young god seated on a goose. He wears the double crown of Upper and Lower Egypt and holds a cornucopia (horn of plenty). On the reverse, a serpent is coiled on an altar. The discovery of this knife handle in the sanctuary has led some scholars to suggest that this structure was dedicated to Harpokrates.

The area, the local name of which is *Ktiston* (structure) was exploited for a long time as a source of ready dressed stone blocks out of which new houses and even terrace walls were built. This activity, aggravated by the recent levelling operations, has led to the almost complete disappearance of the walls and the practically total elimination of the western part of the building. In fact most of what one actually sees to the west of the modern shed belongs to earlier buildings which came to light after the removal of the walls of this later house. What little survives of the walls shows that they were built of dressed stones laid in foundation trenches lined with small rough stones. The lack of walls often makes it difficult to establish the exact limits of a room. These limits are less difficult to determine in rooms where mosaic floors survive, as the edges of the mosaics indicate where the walls once stood. Even here, however, it is often im-

Fig. 2. Knife handle with Harpokrates.

possible to ascertain how one gained access from one room to another. Even more of a problem is the identification of the main entrance into the house which must have been quite imposing. Evidence for a secondary entrance has been found on the north side of the house (Room 20), but a mosaic inscription in the room of the Four Seasons (Room 3) indicates that there was another entrance, probably the main one, near this room on the south, more or less where the modern entrance is located.

The building appears to have been bordered on all four sides by roads, but definite evidence was only forthcoming for the north and south sides. As in many Graeco-Roman houses, the nucleus of the building consists of an atrium (Room 17), a central open court which gave light to the house and around which the most important rooms were grouped. Enough architectural elements survive to show that a colonnaded portico opened on all four sides of the atrium. The roofs of this portico sloped towards the centre, very much in the way that the modern shed has been built, to form the *compluvium,* the purpose of which was to direct rainwater into the atrium where it was collected in an *impluvium.* The water was then directed through underground lead pipes into storage cisterns. Evidence for a complex drainage system has been found in most places where excavation below the mosaic level has been carried out. At least part of the system was connected with the main drain that ran in an E-W direction under the road that flanks the house to the north. It is interesting to note that most mosaic floors incorporated a marble drainhole for collecting the water used for washing them. In the *impluvium* such inlets were equipped with lead strainers.

As it has already been mentioned, the atrium acted as a nucleus around which the important rooms of the house were grouped. Most of these were decorated with mosaics, and, although it is impossible to establish their exact function, if one takes into account the Romans' love of showing off, one can assume that these rooms were open to visitors and guests of the house. More private rooms, like the bedrooms which lie to the east of the atrium (Rooms 21-23), have simpler floors made of small pebbles set in mortar. These floors although not especially attractive, were more than functional and, at least during the cold months of the year, they were in all likelyhood covered with rugs. Even less important rooms such as kitchens and workshops had the simplest of floors made of beaten earth. The bedrooms (Rooms 21-23), kitchens (Rooms 25-27), workshops (Rooms 28-34), baths and latrines (Room 24) lie outside the modern shed.

Apart from the main atrium there are another two open, atrium-like areas. One in the kitchen quarters (Room 19) and another, probably collonaded (Room 18), in the bedroom area. In the middle of the latter there is a deep pond lined with pink hydraulic plaster. Its walls are equipped with small, specially built alcoves in which the fish kept in the pond could enjoy some shade during the hot summer days.

In destroying the walls the stone robbers also destroyed the lavish wall paintings that once decorated them. The little that survived adhering to the lower part of some walls consisted usually of a red band. Enough fragments have been found, however, to show that the walls were once decorated with complex floral and geometric motifs and even figured scenes. A small fragment showing a hand with a bow is exhibited in the Paphos District Museum. In the same museum one can also see several other finds from the house, such as cooking-pots and household vessels found in the kitchen area. There is also a large number of terracotta figurines and moulds from the work-shops, as well as several amphora bases full of lee – all that remains of the wine they once contained. Some spectacular finds from the underlying structures will be mentioned during the description of the mosaics under which they were found (e.g. Rooms 6 and 13).

The house appears to have been built at the very end of the 2nd cent. A.D. and to have been destroyed and abandoned after a series of earthquakes that ruined Paphos and most other towns in Cyprus in the first half of the 4th cent. A.D.

The Mosaics

With the exception of the Scylla mosaic, which has been transferred to Room 1 from an earlier building found under the south-west corner of the portico, all the mosaics seen in the House of Dionysos are in their original position.

Where the bedding of the mosaics was examined, it showed that the method used for laying them was the one commonly employed throughout the ancient world. The ground was levelled and beaten hard. On this surface was laid the *statumen:* a conglomerate of rough stones and coarse mortar. On top of this was laid another layer, the *rudus,* made of crushed stone or gravel and pottery fragments mixed with lime mortar. Finally the *nucleus,* made of very fine plaster, was laid on top, and while this was still wet, the tesserae (small cubes of cut stone) were laid in it and flattened. The

mosaic surface was made more resistant by rubbing marble dust, sand and lime in it, and further levelling was carried out with emery.

The richly coloured tesserae are cut from local stones, except the bright orange, yellow, green and blue ones which are made of glass. Each tessera measures about 1 cubic cm., but smaller ones were also used for the figures where finer detail and definition were called for. The only exception is the geometric mosaic of Room 13 where the tesserae are double the normal size.

It is almost certain that in the period we are dealing with, figure mosaics were not entirely original creative works of art. They were in fact copied, modified, adjusted or combined from copy books which the mosaic workshops had at their disposal and out of which the patron could choose the subjects he wished to have represented in his house. It is often clear that the mosaicists were not particularly well informed about the subjects they were representing. One case in point in the House of Dionysos is the mosaic of Pyramos and Thisbe (first panel of Room 16) where the mosaicist apparently chose the wrong figure and represented Pyramos the river-god (the personification of a river in Asia Minor) rather than the young lover of Thisbe.

The same panel, together with its three companions in the western portico (Room 16), also betrays how scenes of diverse origin were combined to form a unified whole. These four panels are, generally speaking, similar in appearance. In two of them, however, the protagonists are identified by inscriptions while in the other two they are not. There is no reason to presume that explanatory inscriptions were necessary in the first two panels because the

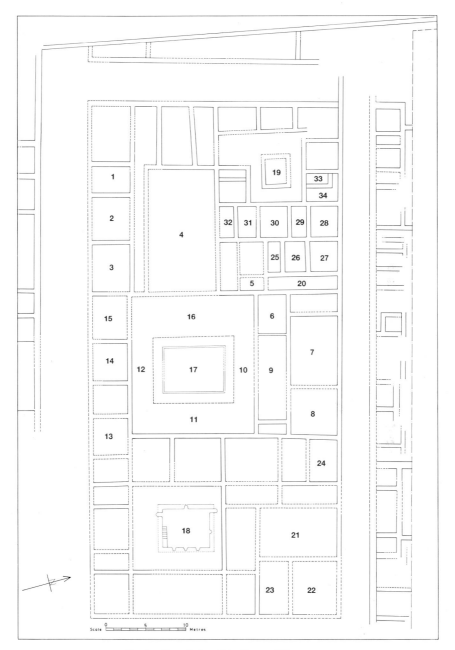

Fig. 3.   Ground plan of the House of Dionysos.

myths they illustrated were more obscure than those in the panels without inscriptions. One has to conclude, therefore, that they do not all derive from one original cycle but from at least two, one with and the other without inscriptions.

Many of these mosaics were copied from earlier mosaics created for different buildings. Such a process is betrayed by the mosaic representing the Rape of Ganymede (Room 8) where the composition ill fits the space available. It was, in fact, found necessary to trim the tips of the eagle's outstretched wings in a rather awkward fashion. This would not have been the case if the composition had been specially created for this room.

When looking at these mosaics one must always bear in mind that in Roman times, especially in the period we are dealing with, most wealthy houses were decorated with mosaic floors. These were made by workshops where most of the work, i.e. geometric frames, background filling, etc., was executed by apprentices or ordinary craftsmen, and only the main figured composition was left to the master craftsman. Creative artists in the modern sense were few and what we are looking at most of the time, is the extremely accomplished work of artisans. This, of course, is not a rule and there are mosaics, which, like several in the House of Dionysos, betray the hand of a real master.

Before proceeding to examine the mosaics individually, it should be emphasized that many of the myths illustrated have been transmitted to us in many different versions. I have chosen the versions that explain the mosaics best, but these are not necessarily the versions of the story that the patron or the mosaicist had in mind. All the passages from Ovid cited in the text come from the translation of his *Metamorphoses* by Mary M. Innes (Penguin Classics, 1964).

The Scylla Mosaic: Room 1 (Fig. 4).

On entering the modern shed, before examining the Roman mosaics, one should look at the Hellenistic floor that now decorates the room on the extreme left. It was found in 1977 during the excavation of trenches for the construction of the shed. It lay about 1 m. below the floor level near the south-west corner of the atrium. This spot is not easily accessible to the general public and for this reason the mosaic was lifted and relaid in this new position so that it can be enjoyed by all visitors to the monument.

Within a geometric frame, a panel measuring 1.32 x 1.22m. is flanked by smaller panels, each with a pair of confronted dolphins. The main panel represents the mythical sea-monster Scylla, part woman, part fish and part dog, described by Homer (*Odyssey*, 12.85ff.) and many other ancient writers. The sad story of "greedy Scylla, girdled with savage dogs barking in the depths of the Sicilian waves" is also recounted in some detail by Ovid (*Metamorphoses*, Book XIV). This horrid monster was once a girl. Glaucus loved her but she did not return his affections. For this reason he sought the help of the sorceress Circe. Unfortunately, Circe was herself in love with Glaucus and on finding her love rejected she tried to eliminate her rival. She mixed magic herbs and juices and poured them in the little bay where Scylla used to rest when the day was at its hottest. Scylla came to the bay and descended into the water up to her waist when the lower part of her body was suddenly transformed into that of

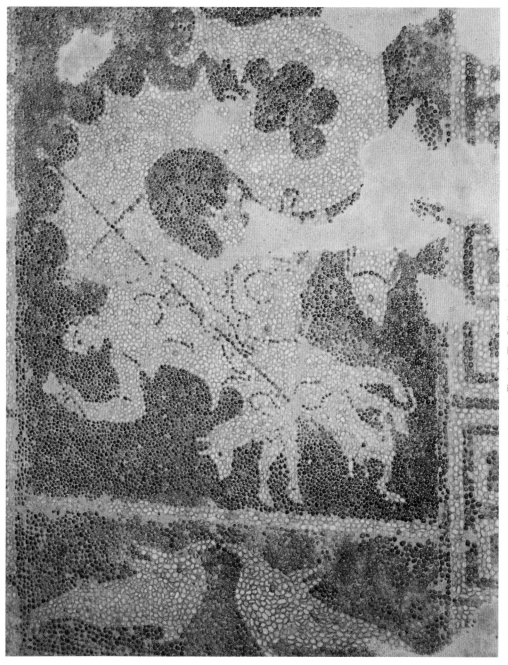

Fig. 4. The Scylla mosaic.

a horrid monster. Scylla never left that bay again and gave vent to her misery by sinking all ships that passed her way.

Scylla is depicted here with a long curving tail ending in crab-like pincers. At the front we see the foreparts of three dogs while waist-up she has the shape of a woman. She is naked and with her right hand raises a long slender instrument, almost certainly a stylized trident, while with her left she holds a mast, presumably from a ship she has just sunk. The dog in the lower left is holding an eel-like creature in his mouth while a larger fish swims freely in the field below.

On grounds of technique and stratigraphy the mosaic has been assigned to the late 4th / early 3rd century B.C., which makes it by far the earliest mosaic known in Cyprus.

The technique in which the mosaic is executed betrays its early date. It is, in fact, totally different from the other mosaics in the building. Instead of being made of specially cut tesserae, as in the later mosaics, it is made of pebbles, used uncut and chosen for their size and colour. The colour palette is very limited and only black and white pebbles are used, except in the hair and the two objects she is holding, where reddish-brown pebbles are employed. Inspite of the limited use of colour the mosaic is of a very high quality and compares favourably with similar mosaics in the rest of the Greek world. The only other known pebble mosaic in Cyprus comes from Kourion but it is of a later date and coarser workmanship, the pebbles being much larger.

Narcissus: Room 2 (Fig. 5).

The first mosaic belonging to the House of Dionysos which the visitor sees, represents Narcissus looking at his reflection in a pool of water. The sad fates of Narcissus and Echo form the subject of one of Ovid's most evocative and touching stories (Book III). When Narcissus, son of the river-god Cephisos and the nymph Liriope, reached the age of sixteen he was so beautiful that many girls and boys fell in love with him. However, his pride and his refusal to return anyone's affections caused endless suffering to those around him. One day when out hunting he was seen by Echo, "that talkative nymph who cannot stay silent when one speaks, but yet has not learned to speak first herself", who fell madly in love with him. Rejected by Narcissus, Echo hid in the woods and mountains never to be seen by anybody again. Tormented by love she became thinner and thinner until all the freshness of her body withered into the air. Finally, only her voice was left, heard by everybody but seen by none.

The cause of so much unhappiness could not remain unpunished, and Narcissus was made to suffer what he himself had caused others to suffer. One day he saw his reflection in a clear pool and immediately fell in love with it. He stayed there admiring himself "at once seeking and sought, himself kindling the flame with which he burned". Gradually, "as golden wax melts with gentle heat, as morning frosts are thawed by the warmth of the sun, so he was worn and wasted away with love, and slowly consumed by its hidden fire". The gods, however, had pity on Narcissus and turned him into a flower that still bears his name and grows near water so that he can always look at his reflection. It is said that his passion continued even after his death, because, when he was received into the underworld, he could not resist admiring his reflection in the waters of

Fig. 5. Narcissus.

the Styx. Both the words narcissism and echo, still in current use, find an explanation of their meaning in this myth.

The mosaic was severely damaged by the levelling operations and has been put together from a large number of fragments. A great part of the geometric decoration is modern.

The Four Seasons: Room 3 (Figs 6-11).

This mosaic was also very badly damaged and its present reconstruction is not necessarily correct. In general lines, the decorative scheme consisted of five panels, each containing a bust, arranged in a quincunx. Only the position of the central and upper left panels is certain since the rest was found in small broken fragments. The busts in the four corners are easily identified as personifications of the Four Seasons because of the attributes they carry with them. The one in the centre, however, is problematic as it has neither attribute nor any specific, recognisable feature (Fig. 6). It is probably Dionysos or Aion or the personification of some concept such as the genius of the Year, all of which are representations that are found associated with the Four Seasons in ancient art.

The bust in the upper left is crowned with ears of corn and holds a sickle (Fig. 7). It can easily be identified as Summer. The one in the upper right represents Spring crowned with flowers and holding a stick (Fig. 8), probably a *pedum* (shepherd's crook). In the lower right we see Autumn holding a badly drawn pruning knife and crowned with leaves and small buds (Fig. 9), and finally in the lower left we see Winter represented as a grey, bearded man (Fig. 10). Next to his head there is an upturned vessel out of which issues water.

The panels between the Seasons represent genre scenes and still lifes, the subjects of which are directly associated with seasonal activities. There is a panel with baskets of grapes and other fruit, one with water fowl and another with vegetables. The best preserved panel shows a goat eating the leaves of a tree (Fig. 11). A bird is perched in the tree and a syrinx (pan-pipes) hangs from one of the branches.

All the panels are framed by a band of solids in perspective, a decorative motif that originated in architecture. It is a generally accepted theory that, in its early stages, mosaic decoration imitated that of ceilings – not only the painted panels in them but also the coffers and other architectural elements that decorated them. One of these elements is the dentil (small square blocks in a row) of Ionic and Corinthian cornices. In the translation from a three-dimensional architectural element to a flat geometric motif the dentils acquired the appearance of solids drawn in perspective. The motif, rendered with varying degrees of competence, was popular throughout ancient mosaic art.

The outer frame of this mosaic includes two *tabulae ansatae* (handled tablets), one containing the inscription XAIPEI (rejoice) and the other KAI CY (you too). Both are forms of wishes of good omen associated with entering or leaving a building and for this reason the room has been identified as an antechamber of the original entrance to the house.

The *Tablinum:* Room 4 (Figs 12-16).

On leaving the room of the Four Seasons one turns left and climbs the wooden bridge that affords a spectacular view of the largest room

Fig. 6. Bust of unidentified figure from the Four Seasons.

Fig. 7. Bust of Summer.

Fig. 8. Bust of Spring.
Fig. 9. Bust of Autumn.

Fig. 10. Bust of Winter.
Fig. 11. Goat panel from the Four Seasons.

in the house. It measures approximately 11.50 x 8.50m. but its western side is very badly damaged. It has been identified as the *tablinum,* a room usually placed at the far end of an atrium. This was the most important room of the house, often with windows opening onto a garden. It was the main reception room and could also be used as a large dining room (*triclinium*). Such use is indicated by the fact that the floor is divided in a manner typical of *triclinia:* immediately inside the entrance there is a very large and elaborately illustrated "doormat" depicting the **Triumph of Dionysos**; and then, further in, the main area of the room has a floor divided into three zones. A large central carpet is decorated with **Vintage scenes** with a multiple view-point so that it could be admired from all sides. This carpet is bordered on three sides (all except the entrance side) by a wide band decorated with a rich geometric pattern formed by peltae (small, light shields, the shape of which had become part of the standard decorative vocabulary). Further out, and again on the same three sides only, a simpler geometric pattern based on the meander runs between the pelta zone and the walls of the room. Unfortunately, both geometric bands are destroyed on the western side.

The reason for this floor division and decoration is the following: when the room was used for dining, the guests, as was the custom of the times, would eat reclining on couches (*klinae*) which were arranged like a Greek Π. In other words they would be covering the area decorated with the pelta pattern. The guests would all be facing towards the centre and would thus have a full view of the richly decorated carpet in the middle. The multiple view-point of the carpet allowed all of them to enjoy it equally whichever side they happened to be

on. The space left between the couches and the walls, i.e. the outer geometric band, was probably used as a corridor through which servants assisting at the banquets could walk without having to pass in front of the guests and disturb them. Such an arrangement was not permanent, however, and the whole room had to be decorated with mosaics for the occasions when it was used for other activities which did not involve the couches.

Both the Triumph of Dionysos and the Vintage scenes are ideal subjects for decorating a dining room.

The Triumph of Dionysos (Fig. 12).

A fair number of examples of Dionysiac processions survive from Antiquity. Many of these illustrate the triumphal return of the god from a military expedition to India whence he brought the Indian slaves and panthers we see on this mosaic. The god, seated on a two-wheeled chariot, occupies the centre of the composition. He wears a crown of ivy leaves and holds a *thyrsus*, a long spear covered with ivy leaves and topped by a pine cone, which was one of the most important attributes of the god and his votaries. Behind him follows a young, tailed Satyr. He is dragging a wineskin, the contents of which he has presumably just emptied in the large crater he is holding, not without some effort, in his left hand. With his left knee he pushes the heavy vessel in an attempt to grip it better. He has, however, been depicted a little too close to Dionysos and his raised leg appears to be resting on the chariot − something that makes no sense since the chariot and the figures are all moving towards the right. Behind the Satyr we see Pan, another of Dionysos' followers. Pan, the god of the woods, half man, half goat, with goat's

Fig. 12. The Triumph of Dionysos.

Figs 13-14. The Dioscouroi.

horns on his forehead, is shown holding a *pedum* (shepherd's crook) and a small shield. Behind him we see an Indian slave, easily recognisable by his dark skin and his hands tied behind his back. There follow two heavily draped Bacchantes, the female followers of Dionysos. The first Bacchante holds a libation bowl in her right hand, and the second, wearing an elaborate crown of flowers, holds a *thyrsus* in her right and the Dionysiac mystic cist in her left. Both *thyrsus* and cist are decorated with ivy leaves.

In front of the god we see two panthers drawing the chariot. Dionysos found the panthers in India and thenceforth they became one of his most important emblems. The reins of the animals are held by Silenus, the oldest member of Dionysos' entourage, whose balding grey head is crowned with ivy leaves. He too holds a

thyrsus covered with ivy leaves. In front of the chariot we see an animal tamer(?), also dark-skinned but of a different hue from that of the Indians. He is turned half-kneeling to face the panthers, and in his extended right hand he holds towards them a strap-like object. The approach of the god is announced by two more of his followers: a Bacchante playing the cymbals, and a naked man. He has an animal skin draped over his shoulder and reeds in his hair, and plays a long trumpet. Between them another Indian, turned towards the advancing god, with his arms raised to his face, appears to be lamenting his misfortunes.

The figures, like those of all the panels, are rendered against a plain white background. Some stand directly on the frame but most are raised above it and stand on individual dark,

Fig. 15. The Vintage Scenes.

shadow-like lines which symbolise the ground — a common convention in Roman mosaics.

The ends of the fillets forming the inside frame of the panel cross each other and project at the corners so as to resemble the overlapping bars of wooden frames (as in an Oxford frame). This is a common expedient, seen elsewhere in the house (e.g. the Peacock panel, Room 15), which was employed either to give the impression of a panel painting or because the mosaic actually copied a panel painting.

The Dioscouroi (Figs 13-14).

On either side of this long frieze there are two small and rather incongruous panels depicting the Dioscouroi, Castor and Pollux. These were the mythical twins that hatched from one of the eggs laid by Leda after her union with Zeus disguised as a Swan (Helen of Troy came out of the other one). They both wear military clothes and hold the reins of a horse that stands behind them. With the other hand they hold a spear. They wear wreaths and a star stands above their heads. The Dioscouroi were endowed with prophylactic powers and were probably put here in order to ward off evil and bring good fortune.

The Vintage Scenes (Figs 15-16).

The superb but alas badly damaged central "carpet" of this room is framed by a luxuriant acanthus scroll inhabited by birds, fruit and flowers. The scroll issues from the beards of large masks that occupy the centre of each side.

The "carpet" itself is a very successful combination of different vignettes played in and

Fig. 16. Peacock and Eros: detail from the Vintage Scenes.

around a network formed by vines laden with grapes. The scenes are half real and half imaginary as humans, horned satyrs and small winged creatures, participate in the activities. Most of them are busy picking grapes, filling baskets and loading them onto donkeys. Intermingled with these scenes there are other portrayals of country life: hunting scenes, a man ready to pounce on a rabbit, a snake coiled around the stem of a vine, a partridge pecking on a bunch of grapes and lots of birds perched on the branches. Along the long axis of the room there appears to have been a line of peacocks that formed the focal point of the composition. Nothing survives of the bird that presumably occupied the western side of the panel. In the centre there is a badly damaged peacock depicted in profile its tail sweeping behind. On the east, opposite the entrance, there is another, splendid peacock shown frontally with its fully spread train held open by a winged Eros (Fig.16).

Small black and white geometric mosaic: Room 5.

Descending the bridge and advancing further north, one sees on one's left the smallest room in the house to have a mosaic floor. It measures only 2.25 x 1.70m. and was the antechamber of the back entrance on the north (Room 20). The simple pattern consists of four-pointed stars separated by lozenges, rendered in black outline against a plain white background.

Phaedra and Hippolytos: Room 6 (Fig. 17).

Turning to the right one faces one of the most important mosaics in the house. It represents

Fig. 17. Phaedra and Hippolytos.

the tragic story of Phaedra and Hippolytos mentioned by several ancient authors and immortalized by Euripides. Theseus, after killing the minotaur with the help of Ariadne, left Crete with her and her sister Phaedra. After abandoning Ariadne, Theseus married the Amazon Antiope who bore him a son named Hippolytos. After the death of Antiope, Theseus married Phaedra. Tormented by a secret love for her stepson, Phaedra finally gave in to her passion and, while her husband was away, sent Hippolytos a written message in which she expressed her sinful love. Hippolytos received the message when he was out hunting and was horrified at what he read. On Theseus' return, Phaedra indignant with unrequited love and frightened at what Hippolytos might do, turned upon him the charge that she deserved. Theseus, outraged at this accusation,

cursed his son and prayed to his father Neptune to punish him. Hippolytos left the town and while riding by the sea a wild bull sent by the god charged out of the water frightening his horses. He was thrown off the chariot and was killed on the rocks. After Hippolytos' unjust death, the truth was revealed and Phaedra, stricken by remorse, killed herself.

The scene depicted on this mosaic is not one of action but one illustrating the calm tension just before the outburst of the tragedy. On the left, Hippolytos accompanied by his dog and naked but for a mantle and hunting boots, stands in an attitude of indecision. He looks almost embarrassed after reading Phaedra's message contained in the diptych he holds in his right hand.

Fig. 18. Mosaic detail from Room 7.

Represented next to him is Phaedra seated on her throne waiting to hear the outcome of her action. The anguish of her passion is illustrated by Cupid flying to the right and lowering his burning torch towards her heart.

When discovered, the floor was in a rather precarious condition and had to be lifted and relaid on a firmer foundation. It was during this operation that an extremely important discovery was made. It was found that the builders of the house, in order to level the ground on which the mosaic was to be laid, filled the depressions in the bedrock with rubbish. This consisted mainly of the ashes and other remains brought from the burnt down Archive

building of Nea Paphos. To our good fortune, together with the ashes came a large number of clay sealings, i.e. the impressions of seals onto wet clay, that were attached to the documents once kept in the Archive. About 11,000 of these were revealed from under the mosaic and they include amongst others a large number of portraits of Ptolemaic kings and Roman emperors and representations of gods.

The Long Room: Room 7 (Fig. 18).

After looking at Phaedra and Hippolytos one should retrace one's steps slightly and proceed further north to a large hall decorated with a polychrome geometric pattern. The design is

Fig. 19. Ganymede and the eagle.

one of the most effective in the house and consists of bands, filled either with a wave motif or a guilloche (plaited ribbons), which intertwin to form a regular succession of small and large circles. These circles and the spaces between them are decorated with a great variety of fillers. These are mostly geometric but they also include many objects and utensils of everyday use. Amongst them are craters, an amphora, a jug and a ladle, several trays (one containing three pomegranates), a garland of flowers and even a silver jug and a mirror. Also worthy of note are the double-axes and the peltae (shields) depicted on the threshold of the room.

The Rape of Ganymede: Room 8 (Fig. 19).

Further to the east one can admire one of the best mosaics of the house. It consists of a small panel set in a field of superimposed octagons and meanders. It represents the moment in which Zeus, in the form of an eagle, carries away young Ganymede.

Ganymede, the shepherd of Ilium (Troy), was considered the most beautiful of all mortals. Not even Zeus could resist his charm. One day, after Hebe the cup-bearer of the gods fell and spilled the nectar, Zeus siezed the opportunity and turning himself into an eagle lifted Ganymede to Olympus to make him the new cup-bearer of the gods. There he "even now mixes the winecups, and supplies Jove with nectar, to the annoyance of Juno" (Ovid, *Metamorphoses*, Book X).

The eagle with wings fully spread is gripping the boy protectively. In his turn Ganymede fastens himself onto the eagle with his hand round the bird's neck. Ganymede is naked but for a cloak and boots. On his head he wears a Phrygian cap (that denotes his place of origin) and in his right hand he holds a spear. On the left, in mid air, we see a pelta that Ganymede has dropped in his confusion.

This is one of the most impressive mosaics but, as we have already said, it is quite clear that a miscalculation on the part of the mosaicist has necessitated the trimming of the tips of the eagle's wings.

The Long Hall: Room 9 (Fig. 20).

Descending the steps and turning to the right, one can admire the floor of another rectangular room which is decorated with a polychrome geometric pattern. This consists of stars of eight lozenges separated by squares. The squares are filled with predominantly geometric motifs, but amongst them there are a few that are filled with objects such as a wreath, a pomegranate, a bunch of grapes, a branch of ivy and a spear, a pelta and a double axe (the last three all together in one square).

The Porticoes to the North, East and South: Rooms 10-12 (Figs 21-24).

Immediately south of the Long Hall, runs the long Northern Portico which, like the porticoes on the east and south of the atrium, is decorated with a hunting scene. Such scenes were among the most popular subjects of ancient

mosaic art. They were particularly popular in North Africa from where they spread to other parts of the Roman Empire. This explains the wealth of exotic beasts illustrated here which are certainly not indigenous to Cyprus and were probably unknown to most of its inhabitants.

The hunters are depicted wearing a variety of boots, short tunics and mantles. The haphazard way in which single animals or groups of animals and hunters are arranged, betrays a derivation from a composition in which the various groups were more logically arranged. The translation of such a composition into the long continuous friezes we have here, has necessitated the illogical but certainly effective way in which the various groups have been arranged.

It should be noted that although the mosaic of the Northern Portico is meant to be viewed

Fig. 20. Mosaic detail from Room 9.

from the atrium side, those of the other two porticoes are meant to be viewed from the inside of the house.

The Northern Portico: Room 10.

A tree at one end of the panel and another next to a rocky prominence, close to the centre, establish the setting in which the hunt is taking place. At the other end a city gate or pavilion closes the scene. Between these three elements we see several episodes: on the west a hunter is ready to confront a lion with a spear. Nearby, another hunter with raised hand is ready to strike a rampant wild boar with a club. On the other side of the hillock we see a headless onager with blood pouring out of its truncated neck. The onager looks as if it is about to collapse on the ground but, from similar representations elsewhere we know that it should be understood as already dead and lying on its side. In front of it a leopard advances rather sedately, holding in its mouth the head of the unfortunate creature (Fig. 21). This rather unpleasant and gruesome scene was, quite surprisingly, a popular element in Roman decoration and is found in several mosaics in other parts of the Roman world.

The Eastern Portico: Room 11.

Animals and hunters are shown again running in different directions in a landscape set by trees, rocks and an altar-like structure in the centre. First we see a tiger chasing a wild boar, then a bear and then a hunter attacking a leopard with a spear (Fig. 22). Further on and running in the opposite direction we see a dog chasing two moufflons — the only wild animal depicted that is indigenous to Cyprus (Fig. 23). Finally we see a hunter about to spear an unfortunate wild donkey whose leg is already caught between the jaws of a fierce hunting dog.

The Southern Portico: Room 12.

Different animals are depicted in this panel. First we see a half-kneeling hunter ready to spear a bull that charges towards him. Beyond a tree we see another hunter armed with a spear about to attack a lion. Separated by a tree, we next see a dog confronting a deer and then, after an altar and a tree, we see a running tiger (Fig. 24). The scene closes with another tree.

Before proceeding to visit the Western Portico with its mythological scenes, one should retrace one's steps and examine some of the mosaics in the smaller rooms of the southern wing.

Black and White Geometric Floor: Room 13.

The easternmost paved room of the south wing has what is certainly the most plain mosaic of the house. Its rather uninteresting pattern of little white squares forming a trellis against a black background is made even coarser by the size of the tesserae: they are, twice as large as those in the other rooms, and measure about 2 cubic cm. This plain mosaic, however, concealed one of the site's greatest treasures. During the digging of a foundation trench to the north of the room, workmen came across an amphora buried about 45cm. below the mosaic floor and containing 2484 silver Ptolemaic tetradrachms — the biggest Ptolemaic hoard ever found in Cyprus. The coins are in excellent condition and date to the period between 204 and 88 B.C. They originate from the Cypriot mints of Salamis, Kition and Paphos, except for one group which, although bearing the

Fig. 21. Leopard from Northern Portico.
Fig. 22. Hunter attacking leopard from Eastern Portico.

Fig. 23. Moufflon from Eastern Portico.
Fig. 24. Tiger from Southern Portico.

Fig. 25. Multiple geometric panels.

mint-marks of Paphos, was minted in Alexandria. The amphora with the coins was obviously hidden some time in the 1st century B.C. and there it remained, escaping discovery by the builders that worked on the spot at different periods.

Mosaic with Multiple Geometric Panels: Room 14 (Fig. 25).

After a room with a simple earthen floor we come to a very effective geometric mosaic. It consists of four rows of four panels, each containing a different geometric pattern. All the patterns used are well known and quite standard to the Roman decorative vocabulary. They owe their effect here to the beautiful colour scheme and the fact that they are exhibited all together like a page from a sample book. This kind of decoration, known as "à décor multiple" was very common in the western Roman provinces, particularly in France, and it is only rarely found among eastern mosaics.

The Room of the Peacock: Room 15 (Fig. 26).

Between Room 14 and that of the Four Seasons (Room 3) there is a smallish room decorated with an elaborate geometric pattern, in the middle of which there is a panel depicting a peacock. The bird stands frontally on a strip of ground against a white background that highlights the intense blue of its fully spread train. The whole panel is framed by a band of guilloche, but, further in, there is another, narrower frame of a type we have already seen (Room 4, Triumph of Dionysos) which imitates the frame of a panel painting.

The Western Portico: Room 16 (Figs 27-34).

Turning right after the Room of the Peacock one enters the Western Portico. Its decoration is in marked contrast to that of the other three porticoes. Whilst each of these had a single long panel with hunting scenes, the Western Portico is divided into four rectangular panels. Three are of more or less equal size but the fourth (the second from the left) is almost twice as long as the others. This expedient was carefully worked out so that this long panel would lie in front of the *tablinum* (Room 4) and have its centre on the axis of this room. Moreover, the subject matter of the long panel, the story of **Icarios and Dionysos,** is a very apt subject for what was in effect an antechamber to the dining room, and contrasts with that of the other three panels which illustrate mythical love stories.

The geometric pattern all round this portico consists of crosses separated by octagons. These contain geometric fillers but above and below the Icarios panel they are highlighted by Dionysiac masks (satyrs, maenads, Silenus) and birds – thus emphasizing the relation of this panel to the *tablinum.*

Pyramos and Thisbe (Figs 27-28).

The first panel on the left represents the story

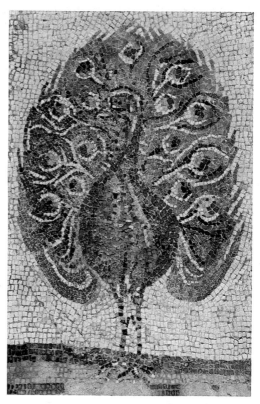

Fig. 26. The Peacock in Room 15.

of Pyramos and Thisbe, immortalized by Ovid (*Metamorphoses*, Book IV) and made more familiar to modern readers by Shakespeare's use of it in "Midsummer Night's Dream". The story in its general lines is also very similar to another of Shakespeare's plays, "Romeo and Juliet". In the words of Ovid, "Pyramus was the most handsome of young men and Thisbe the fairest beauty of the East". They lived in Babylonia and were neighbours. They loved each other tenderly but, as they came from hostile families, they had to keep their love secret. They used, in fact, to communicate through a crack in the wall that separated their

Fig. 27. Pyramos and Thisbe.

houses. One day, "when Aurora had put out night's starry fires and the sun's rays had dried the frosty grass, they came to their usual meeting place". After lamenting their sad lot they resolved to meet at night, outside the city gates. They agreed to meet under a mulberry tree that grew by a spring next to Ninus' tomb.

Thisbe, her face hidden under a veil, arrived at the spot first and sat waiting for her lover under the mulberry tree which was laden with white fruit. Suddenly, a lioness fresh from the kill, her jaws dripping with blood, came to quench her thirst at the spring. Thisbe, frightened, rushed into a nearby cave but in her flight dropped her veil which the lioness took and ripped apart with her bloody jaws.

On approaching the meeting place, Pyramos noticed the animal's footprints and his worst fears were confirmed when he saw the blood-stained veil. Thinking Thisbe dead and unable to contain his unhappiness, Pyramos drew his sword and thrust it into his side. Then, with one last effort, he pulled it out of the wound. His blood spouted forth and sprinkled the fruit on the tree turning it to a dark purple colour.

Meanwhile, Thisbe, recovering from her fright, came out of her hiding place and was confronted with Pyramos' body. In her horror and despair she took his sword and threw herself on it. Before dying she begged that their bodies be buried in a single tomb, and that the tree under which the tragedy was unfolded would bear fruit of a dark and mournful hue in memory of their hapless love. In fact, as Ovid assures us, the ashes of the two lovers rest together in a single urn and ever since then the berries of the mulberry tree always turn a dark purple colour when ripe.

Fig. 28. Thisbe.

What we actually see in the mosaic is the moment when Thisbe (Fig. 28), panic stricken, is rushing to hide from the wild beast — a leopard, not Ovid's lioness. Opposite her we find not Thisbe's lover but the figure of a river-god with the name Pyramos written above it. He is represented in the typical attitude of a river deity: half reclining against an upturned jug out of which water issues profusely. His head is crowned with weeds while in his left hand he holds a reed. In his extended right arm he holds a cornucopia (horn of plenty), the symbol of the river's beneficial effect on agriculture. As we have said earlier on, we are here witnessing a mistake on the part of the mosaicist who, instead of representing Thisbe's lover, represented another Pyramos, a river in Cilicia in Asia Minor (mentioned by Strabo, XII.2.4).

Icarios and Dionysos (Figs 29-32).

Further to the right we see the largest panel of the portico, representing the story of Icarios. According to some ancient authors Icarios was king of Athens but according to others he was a gardener — which is what he appears to be on our mosaic. Icarios offered hospitality to Dionysos when the latter was visiting Athens and in return the god taught him how to cultivate the vine and make wine out of its fruit, introducing in this way viticulture to mankind. He warned him, however, to hide his wine well, otherwise disasters would befall himself and his family. Unfortunately, Icarios did not heed the god's advice and, while returning home with his first vintage, offered some shepherds that happened to be passing by some of his precious liquor. The shepherds became intoxicated and, thinking themselves poisoned, attacked and killed Icarios. This was a sad end indeed for the first man to make wine, and the story, as we shall see, was probably chosen, on purpose, because of its moral message, for decorating this part of the portico.

The scene represented on the mosaic is the moment just before the tragedy. In the centre, Icarios (Fig. 29) is holding the reins of an ox-driven cart loaded with animal-skins containing wine (Fig. 30). Further to the right we see two men designated by an inscription as "the first wine drinkers". One of them, overcome by wine is on the ground leaning against a wine-skin. The other is still managing to hold himself up and drink out of a cup.

Fig. 29. Icarios.

On the left-hand side, the god of wine himself, Dionysos, is seated on a stool, holding a bunch of grapes (Fig. 31). He appears to be offering it to the nymph Akme who is seated opposite him drinking wine out of a bowl (Fig. 32). Both figures are crowned with vine leaves and grapes. Akme is by no means a well known figure in Greek mythology but her identification is made certain by the inscription above her head. The name in Greek means culmination or perfection (usually of age) and one cannot avoid interpreting her presence here as symbolic. If this is the case, she would stand for the state of mind brought about by the proper and moderate use of wine. In fact Icarios seems to be pointing towards her in quite a meaningful manner. The two drunk shepherds on the other side would then symbolize the evils that improper use of wine leads to. This is of course only a hypothesis, but one cannot resist giving this interpretation to a mosaic that had to be crossed before one entered into the dining room.

Neptune and Amymone (Fig. 33).

The next panel, like the last one to the right, has no explanatory inscriptions but its interpre-

Fig. 30. Oxen and cart.

Fig. 31. Dionysos.

Fig. 32. Akme.

Fig. 33. Neptune and Amymone.

tation is not particularly difficult. It illustrates the myth of Neptune and Amymone, of which there exist many variations. In general lines, the story is the following: Neptune, to revenge himself for losing Argolis (an area in Greece) to Hera, dried up all the rivers and springs of the area. Danaos sent his fifty daughters, one of whom was Amymone, to search for water advising them to do everything in their power to placate the god's anger. During her search Amymone saw a deer and aimed at it with her bow. She missed, however, and the arrow fell near a sleeping Satyr who woke up and tried to ravish her. Suddenly Neptune appeared and chased the Satyr away with his trident. The god of water was immediately attracted to Amymone, and she, remembering her father's words, gladly gave herself to him. The god, in return, revealed to her the spring of Lerna thus bringing an end to the terrible drought.

The mosaic illustrates the moment when Neptune, after having got rid of the Satyr, ad-

vances, trident in hand, towards Amymone. Cupid hovers between the two figures with a torch in his right hand and a rectangular parasol in his left which he stretches towards Amymone. In the lower foreground, a metal jug reminds us of the original purpose of Amymone's wanderings.

Apollo and Daphne (Fig. 34).

The last panel illustrates the myth of Apollo and Daphne, one of the most well known and loved myths of Antiquity. There are no inscriptions to explain the action but no one would have had any difficulty in identifying the protagonists. The nymph Daphne, daughter of the river Peneus, had sworn eternal chastity. The god Apollo, however, fell in love with her and after failing to convince her to consent to his wishes, tried to catch her by force. "Thus the god and the nymph sped on, one made swift by hope and one by fear; but he who pursued was swifter, for he was assisted by love's

Fig. 34. Apollo and Daphne.

wings" (Ovid *Metamorphoses*, Book I). In their mad chase they reached the waters of Peneus and just as Apollo was about to catch his victim, Daphne prayed to her father for help. All of a sudden, her feet remained rooted to the ground, her body was covered by bark, and her arms and hair turned into branches and leaves. She had, in fact, turned into a laurel tree, a plant that in Greek still bears her name, Daphne. Apollo continued to love Daphne even after her metomorphosis. For this reason he chose the laurel to be his sacred tree, and his garlands were henceforth made with its leaves. He also granted that just as his head was ever young, so should the tree always be green and never lose its foliage.

On the mosaic we see the moment when Daphne is rooted to the ground, her legs turning into a tree. She is standing next to her father Peneus, represented as a river deity in the fashion we have already seen in the panel of Pyramos and Thisbe. To the right, Apollo, still running with bow in hand, points with amazement at the transformation. His arrows, still in the quiver, can be seen behind his right shoulder.

D.M.

THE HOUSE OF ORPHEUS

The House of Orpheus is situated to the west of the Villa of Theseus (Fig. 1). Although the site has been known for a long time its systematic excavation started only five years ago. In 1942 British soldiers excavating trenches for air-raid shelters, came across a mosaic representing Hercules and the Lion — the first mosaic to be discovered in Paphos! Although the mosaic was photographed, the floor and its location were subsequently forgotten. In 1963 the late K. Nicolaou dug some trial trenches in order to locate it, but instead he came across another mosaic, representing an Amazon. The site was again covered up unitl 1978 when Nicolaou tried again to find the Hercules mosaic, this time successfully. It was then realized that this mosaic and the Amazon panel were, in fact, part of one and the same floor. The Hercules mosaic prompted Nicolaou to name the building the 'House of Hercules'. The mosaic was fully recorded and covered up again until 1982 when the systematic excavation of the building was undertaken by the present writer. In 1984, following the discovery of a very important mosaic of Orpheus, the name of the house was changed to that of the new hero.

The Building (Fig. 35).

Although an area of about 600 square metres has already been excavated, it is still too early for the plan of the building to be intelligible. It appears to be of traditional type, however, with a colonnaded atrium around which the

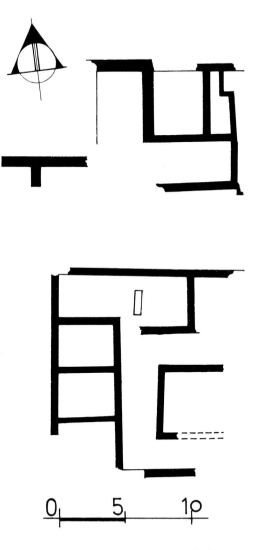

Fig. 35. Ground plan of the House of Orpheus.

46

Fig. 36. Hercules and the Lion of Nemea.

rooms are arranged. Recent (1987) investigations near the NE corner of the site have brought to light the edge of a group of rooms that almost certainly belongs to the bath complex of the house. Stone robbing and the World War II air-raid shelters have disturbed the site considerably, especially towards the west of the excavated area where the mosaics are located. On the east side the walls survive to a fair height and are often faced with plaster. This is scored in herring-bone fashion in order to provide better adherence for the final layer of painted plaster that once decorated the house. Myriads of fragments of painted wall plaster have been found in the debris and it is hoped that it will be possible to reconstruct at least part of the decorative scheme of the building.

The surviving walls show two distinct building phases. Small scale excavation below the floor level has shown that one of these phases belongs to an earlier underlying building of a slightly different plan. With the exception of the three mosaic rooms, all other rooms in the house have floors of beaten earth or, as in the case of those in the bath complex, of high quality cement. The date of the last phase of the house will be established once the excavation material has been studied systematically. For the moment, a date in the late 2nd / early 3rd cent. A.D. seems the most probable.

The Mosaics

Only three rooms with mosaic floors have been discovered so far. The figured mosaics are quite similar in style and technique to those of the House of Dionysos. The stones used are again local except that here, both in the background of the Amazon panel and in the frame of the Orpheus mosaic, the tesserae are

Fig. 37. The Amazon.

made of a grey-blue marble of a type not found on Cyprus.

A repeating polychrome pattern of peltae covers the entire floor. In it are inserted two panels: a small rectangular one opposite the threshold and a larger one with an Amazon further in near the centre. The position of this panel is problematic since it is neither in the centre of the room nor on any of its axes.

Hercules and the Lion of Nemea (Fig. 36).

This is a straightforward depiction of Hercules' first labour in which he killed the invulnerable Lion of Nemea, in order to take its skin to king Eurystheus. The Lion of Nemea was a mythical beast that, according to some, was born to Echidna and Orthros, and according to others, fell from the moon. Hercules first tried his arrows but to no effect. He then chased it

Fig. 38. Orpheus and the Beasts.

with his club but the Lion hid in a cave. After blocking one of the two exits of the cave, Hercules entered, threw his club away and throttled the beast with his bare hands.

The mosaic depicts the moment when Hercules and the Lion are about to engage in the fight and in this it is very unusual since traditional iconography represents the two of them already fully engaged in the fight. The demigod is represented completely naked with his club discarded to the left of the panel.

The Amazon (Fig. 37).

The Amazons were daughters of Mars and Harmonia (or Mars and Venus) and lived in a country of their own in Asia Minor, entirely populated by women. In order to preserve their race they mated once a year with their neighbours and of the children born they only kept the girls. The boys they either killed, castrated or returned to their fathers. They were a beautiful but war-loving race that usually fought on horseback and carried the characteristic double-axe.

Our Amazon stands holding the reins of her horse in an unusual attitude, very reminiscent of that of the Dioscuroi in the House of Dionysos. Nothing remains of the barbaric clothes Amazons usually wear in earlier representations except for the Phrygian cap and

Fig. 39. Orpheus and the inscription.

the boots. In her left hand she holds a double-axe.

Hercules' ninth labour was to procure the golden girdle of Ares worn by Hippolyte, queen of the Amazons. It is impossible to say whether the panel here depicts Hippolyte herself, and is to be associated with Hercules in the nearby panel, or whether it is an independent representation of an Amazon.

Orpheus and the Beasts (Figs 38-39).

This mosaic decorates a room measuring 4.25 x 5.10m. Apart from a rather simple geometric frame, the whole floor is occupied by one large panel. Orpheus is seated on a rock and with his left hand holds a lyre, the sounds of which attract a multitude of creatures that gather enchanted around him. With his right hand he holds the plectrum and with his finger he indicates the effect his music has on the animals. The magic of Orpheus' music is also known from two other myths. The most famous is the rescue of his wife Eurydice from the Underworld after Orpheus had enchanted Hades and Persephone with his songs. The other refers to the safe passage of the Argonauts from the dreaded Sirens, whose calls Orpheus drowned with his music.

Orpheus is clad in elaborate clothes and wears a Phrygian cap (Fig. 39). The beasts around him are (starting from the bottom left) a fox, a bear and a boar. On a higher register there is a seated cow, a leopard and a lion. Behind the cow there is a partridge, while on Orpheus' left there is a tiger and on his right a deer. Next to the rock there is a large coiled snake. Higher up on the left there is an eagle, a peacock and fragments of another bird, while on the right there is a parrot(?) and the legs of yet another bird that cannot be identified.

The most important feature of this mosaic is the inscription that runs above Orpheus. It reads [ΤΙΤ]ΟΣ (or [ΓΑΙ]ΟΣ) ΠΙΝΝΙΟΣ ΡΕΣΤΙΤΟΥΤΟΣ ΕΠΟΙΕΙ, in other words, "Titus (or Gaius) Pinnius Restitutus made it". This, however, does not necessarily mean that Restitutus was the artist that made the mosaic. In the period we are dealing with, to make something could equally well signify to pay for something to be made. In this case then, Titus Pinnius Restitutus would be the owner of the house. Whichever the exact meaning, such inscriptions are not all that common and this is the first one we know of from Roman Cyprus. It is interesting to note that although written in Greek characters, the name is Latin.

The south wall of the room survives to a fair height and preserves a red painted dado. The many fragments of painted wall plaster found on the mosaic show that higher up, the walls were much more elaborately decorated. This same south wall has a small hole through which the water used for cleaning the floor was piped (and still is) into one of the main drains of the house.

The Monochrome Geometric Mosaic.

In 1986 a third mosaic floor was discovered near the SW limit of the excavated area. It is not a figured representation but a geometric design. It is, however, of a most rare and interesting type as its decoration is entirely monochrome and the patterns are traced out, not by colour but by the way the tesserae are set in the mortar. The colour is pale greenish grey and the design consists of octagons (containing concentric circles) separated by small squares. The central field is bound by a series of borders made of rows of tesserae set alternatingly parallel and diagonal to the frame.

The mosaic lay just below modern ground level and it was, unfortunately, very badly damaged by ploughing when this part of Paphos was under cultivation. The plough has also removed all stratified material lying on top of the floor, something that makes its dating very problematic. In appearance, the mosaic seems to be slightly later than the other mosaics in the house.

D.M.

THE VILLA OF THESEUS

The discovery and subsequent excavation.

In 1965 the Polish Archaeological Mission of the University of Warsaw began the systematic study of the south-western zone of the ancient city. Work concentrated in the area known as *Maloutena* located about 250m. west of the port and about 100m. south of the House of Dionysos (Fig. 1). The first season of excavations brought to light statuettes of Asclepios and Artemis. In the following years the collection of statues and statue fragments increased. Furthermore, excavations uncovered the remains of city buildings dating from at least the end of the 4th century B.C. to the Roman period. Work carried out in 1966 led to the discovery of the first traces of a Roman building which surpassed in size the usual standards found in city buildings. The building is now known as the **Villa of Theseus,** after the mosaic representation of the Athenian hero shown fighting the Minotaur. Due to its large proportions the building has not yet been completely uncovered.

The Building
(all room numbers refer to Fig. 40).

Archaeological evidence suggests that the construction of the villa probably started in the second half of the 2nd century A.D. upon ruins of earlier houses of the Hellenistic and early Roman periods. The building existed until at least the early 7th century A.D., but in its final period was occupied by squatters who caused great damage to the once rich decoration of the rooms. Traces of squatter occupation are visible in various places in the form of lime kilns (in Room 44), circular ovens (in Rooms 40-41, 65), and small compartments (Room 28). The plan of the villa, inspired by Hellenistic tradition, is that of a peristyle building. There are four wings each comprised of several rows and rooms, situated on the four sides of a large central court which probably had colonnaded porticoes on three sides: the south, the west and the east. The floor of all three porticoes was decorated throughout with geometric mosaics while the courtyard was left unpaved. The edifice grew horizontally rather than vertically, covering several *insulae* (blocks of houses) of the existing grid of Hellenistic streets. It measures over 120m. east to west and over 80m. north to south. In the later Roman period a new street had to be opened along its eastern façade. Only in some parts was the building provided with an upper storey (see stairs in Rooms 21 and 53). The villa underwent many alterations and enlargements, particularly in the course of the 4th century A.D. Its initial plan, however, displays a clearly defined division of functions. The official and the domestic parts are well separated. The plan, the size, the rich decoration, marble statues, marble revetment of walls, fine mosaics and wall paintings, and a Latin inscription which is very rare in Greek-speaking Cyprus, and mentions the execution of porticoes, suggest that the edifice served as a *villa publica,* an official residence, possibly for the governors / proconsuls of the province of Cyprus. The Villa of Theseus is the largest residential structure of its type found on the island so far and one of the largest in the Mediterranean.

East Wing (Fig. 40).

The visitor approaches the villa from the east, the same direction taken by the main road from the port to the palace in antiquity. The monumental entrance complex was on the axis of this street. A wooden walkway for tourists has now been constructed along this axis. The entrance complex is of special interest: it incorporates several architectural ideas deriving from different traditions, both Greek and Italian. Through a large gate once flanked by columns, the visitor enters into a large vestibule (no. 69) provided with benches. This room is 22.5m. long and 5.20m. wide with semicircular apses at both ends. The floor is decorated with a mosaic made up of simple geometric patterns. The walls had been plastered with a white lime plaster. Three entrances lead from this vestibule into the palace; the centre one is the main public entry into the atrium (nos 71-72). The side entrances led to the household and dwelling areas (on the south to Room 92 and on the north to Room 93). The main entry to the atrium was further accentuated by the presence of niches on either side. One would expect decorative statuary to have been placed there. The atrium was of the tetrastyle type reminiscent of such atria in Pompeii and Herculaneum. The roof which sloped down inside, was supported on four columns or pillars standing in the corners of a rectangular pool (*impluvium*) revetted with marble slabs. Light entered through an opening (*compluvium*) in the centre of the roof. Rain-water was gathered in the pool beneath. Any surplus water was drained through pipes into the storage cisterns.

Matching the four columns or pillars supporting the roof of the atrium were decorative pilasters set in pairs on the northern and southern walls of the atrium. The walls were decorated with figural paintings, traces of which have been preserved in the eastern end of the room. Contrary to earlier Italian tradition, the atrium of the Villa of Theseus did not communicate with side rooms, but only with the eastern portico of the main peristyle court. On the floor of the atrium there was a geometric mosaic, the key motif of which was a red-claret maeander on a light background. The mosaic, which was used over a long period of time, shows evidence of repairs, especially near the entrance. Of interest is the fact that in repairing the mosaic in antiquity specialists introduced completely new patterns which had nothing to do with the original decoration. This created the impression that a new carpet with different motifs had been placed on top of the old threadbare one. The deep niche in the western part of the atrium probably contained some statuary. Behind the niche there was a small *nymphaeum* (water fountain) provided with three basins and revetted with marble slabs. Upon crossing the atrium, the visitor had an imposing view of the large inner courtyard (46 x 38m.) lined on east, south and west

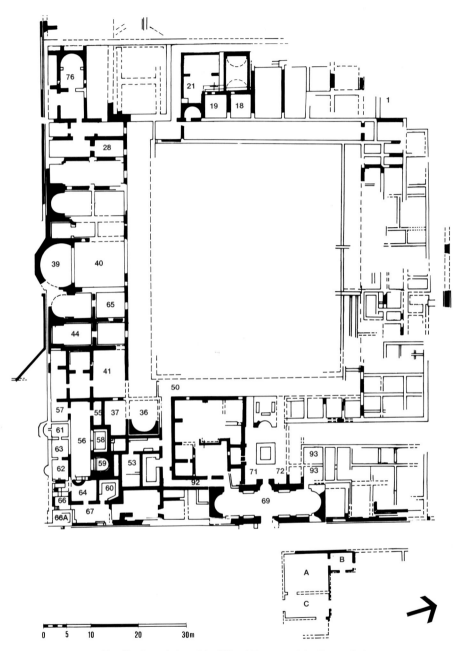

Fig. 40. Ground plan of the Villa of Theseus and the House of Aion.

with the marble colonnades of three porticoes, the floors of which were decorated with fine geometric mosaics. Best preserved is the mosaic of the eastern portico (no. 50), about 42m. long.

South Wing (Fig. 40).

The south wing was the oldest and the richest part of the villa. It was provided with a 56m. long and 5.5m. wide colonnaded portico paved throughout with a geometric mosaic. Onto the portico opened a series of stately rooms and apsidal halls reminiscent of similar rooms in Roman palaces in Italy, Germany, or in rich Roman villas of Spain, France and England. They were used for official purposes and for decorative display. In the centre is to be found the main hall (nos 39-40) composed of a slightly elevated horseshoe-shaped apse and a rectangular lower chamber. This was the principal reception and audience room. One of the figural mosaics (see below, Achilles mosaic) is to be seen in the lower part of the room. The plan of the hall brings to mind throne rooms of imperial palaces. Another stately room (no. 36), which probably had a recreational character, is located at the east end of the portico. It contains the most beautiful of all the mosaics found within the villa (see below, Theseus mosaic).

After passing through the Theseus room the modern walkway leads to a luxurious bath complex (nos 56-67) in the south-east corner of the edifice. The bath, which is composed of many rooms, was built on a plan characteristic of private thermal establishments intended for a limited number of users. Unlike the big Imperial baths, which usually had a one-way circuit for the bathers, here the users of the bath had to retrace their steps through the various parts of the establishment. A large *frigidarium* (cold room), decorated with a fine geometric mosaic, occupies the centre (no. 56). Two big basins (nos 58-59) for cold ablutions were located on its north side: originally they were revetted with marble slabs and decorated with marble sculptures. On the east side of the cold room another basin for foot-washing was added at a later period. The heated part was placed on the south side. Hot air distributed from the nearby oven (no. 66) heated the hypocaust floors of the *tepidarium* (no. 61, moderately heated room), *sudatorium* (no. 63, steam bath), and *caldarium* (no. 62, warm bath). The bath had two *apodyteria* (nos 64,55?) (dressing rooms), a *cella unctuaria* for anointments (no. 57?), a latrine (no. 60) for 12-14 people at a time and an elevated water tank (no. 66A). All rooms were embellished with floor mosaics, murals and marble revetment for walls and basins. The bath was provided with a complicated system of drains and pipes. Used water from the cold basins was directed though channels to flush the latrine. During their long existence the baths underwent numerous alterations and in their final years became accessible also to people from outside the villa.

West Wing (Fig. 40).

The west wing was probably used as residential quarters and storage areas. Here, in Rooms 18, 19 and near Room 1, many marble statues of gods, goddesses and heroes were found. Most of them could be assigned to the late 2nd / early 3rd century A.D. They include Dionysos (Bacchus), god of wine; two statues of Aphrodite (Venus), goddess of love; Artemis (Diana), the divine huntress; Asclepios, supreme master of medicine, feeding with an egg the snake that coils around his staff (Fig. 41). They were accompanied by Persephone, wife of Hephaestos, god of the Underworld, a satyr, a silenus, and Heracles, the invincible hero; also a number of other statues in fragmentary condition, among them a beautiful head of the Egyptian goddess Isis (Fig. 42). All these sculptures are now on display in the Paphos District Museum. All except one were made of white marble, usually imported from the Greek islands of the Aegean. Probably in the latter part of the 4th century A.D. a second court at the rear west side of the wing and a watchtower, were incorporated into the palace enclosure.

North Wing (Fig. 40).

The north wing was composed of small rooms for servants and slaves, workshops and laundries which were provided with waterproof floors and pear-shaped water cisterns several meters deep. On the north, the wing was bordered by a passage or street about 3m. wide with a water drain running down the middle. The north wing has been very badly damaged by stone robbers quarrying the ready-made building material and by long-term cultivation. Most of the walls visible at present belong to an earlier phase of building activity in the area, a phase preceding the construction of the palace.

The Mosaics.

More than 1400 square metres of mosaic pavements have been found within the building which occupies an area of about 9600 square metres. Most of these mosaics bear elaborate geometric motifs of fine workmanship. Only about 10% of the decorated surface is taken up by figural panels. This proportion is not excep-

Fig. 41. Statue of Asclepios.

tional for Paphos: it represents a normal practice in the Roman world due to the elevated cost of the execution of figural compositions.

In contrast to the House of Dionysos (see above), where all the mosaics were made at approximately the same time, the mosaic decoration within the Villa of Theseus belongs to various periods ranging from the late 3rd to the 5th century A.D. The technique does not differ from other mosaics in Paphos except that in some figural scenes, in addition to the tesserae made of local stones which constitute the bulk of the material, more glass cubes have been used for the rare colours. For some figural representations much smaller tesserae were used (2-5mm.) than any known from other Paphos mosaics. With such large areas decorated with mosaics, most of the floors must have been executed by common apprentices working under the supervision of a qualified foreman. Mosaic workshops gathered many different specialists: the better paid craftsmen of wall mosaics and the less prized ones of geometric floor mosaics who copied previously prepared designs. There were also mosaicists specializing in the execution of figural scenes. Althrough they seldom signed their work, they left behind them pictures surpassing in quality the correctness of average representations. One of these exceptional mosaics can be seen in the Villa of Theseus.

Theseus Mosaic: Room 36 (Fig. 43).

The mosaic decorates Room 36 which lies directly on the longitudinal axis of the south portico of the palace. It is the culminating point of the geometric mosaic floor of the portico itself. The room is almost square (6 x 5.50m.). Its rear wall forms a spacious apse once revetted with marble slabs. The decoration of the pave-

Fig. 42. Head of Isis.

ment is especially well suited to the shape of the room. The two front corners, in the shape of triangles, are filled with a floral ornament: yellow-white lilies bend down to the ground, and are contrasted against the dark claret background. The flowers are rendered with a remarkable freshness in a highly pictorial though not naturalistic way. The remaining part of the floor forms a circle in the centre of which there is a medallion (2.20m. in diameter) containing a representation of the mythical duel between Theseus and the Minotaur in the Labyrinth on Crete (Fig. 43).

Theseus, an Athenian hero, was the son of the

god of the sea, Poseidon, or of king Aegeus of Athens and the Troezen princess Aethra. As a youth, already famous for his deeds, Theseus decided to accompany to Crete the Athenian hostages who were sent to Knossos every seven years as prey for the Minotaur, the cruel half man, half bull living in the depths of the Labyrinth. This painful tribute had been forced upon the Athenians by the Cretan king Minos. The youth decided to fight the monster. Upon arriving in Crete he was helped by Ariadne, daughter of king Minos, who fell in love with the handsome prince. She told Theseus how to enter the Labyrinth and gave him a ball of thread so that he could mark the difficult way back through the corridors of the maze. Theseus killed the Minotaur, thereby freeing the hostages, and sailed away from Crete together with Ariadne.

The scene on the mosaic shows a decisive moment in the fight. Unlike most of the other mosaics with this subject known from various parts of the Roman Empire, the Paphos representation does not limit itself to the main protagonists, i.e. Theseus and the Minotaur alone. In the centre, within a dark cave, there stands the young hero holding a club in his right hand. With the left he grasps the horn of the monster who has already fallen to his knees. An old man, god of the Labyrinth, is seated on the ground; he looks on at the combat, a horrified look on his face. From above the rocks overhanging the cave, Ariadne and another woman, a personification of Crete with a turretted crown upon her head, greet the victorious hero. Besides the cave, which can be understood as the depths of the Labyrinth, the Cretan maze is represented on the mosaic in yet another way in the form of the magnificent frame around the figural scene. This frame is made up of two fairly simple geometric ornaments: a chain of dark claret and light blue diamonds and a multicolored guilloche. Rows of diamonds form a series of ever smaller circles which, however, are not closed. Each of them is divided into segments as if to leave a sinuous path in between. Through these complicated passages runs a guilloche – Ariadne's thread – showing the way out of the dwelling of the Minotaur. It leads from around the central medallion to the threshold of the room.

Archaeological evidence indicates that the pavement was created at the very end of the 3rd or in the early 4th century A.D. However, the figural scene had suffered damage, possibly during one of the earthquakes of the 4th century A.D., and had to be restored sometime later, probably in the last quarter of that century. Only stylistic differences (if one disregards the evidence of the mortar bedding) testify to these repairs executed by expert craftsmen, representing great artistic skill. The heads and upper parts of the bodies of Theseus and Crete were remade. The upper part of the medallion between Ariadne and Crete was also altered, a plain white background substituting, most probably, the heads of the Athenian hostages who could have been represented there observing the combat from behind some rocks. The god of the Labyrinth and Ariadne, who belong to the first period, are still close to an early stylistic tradition going back to Hellenistic times. The heads of Theseus and Crete, on the other hand, reveal the style of the approaching Byzantine era. They recall the faces of Christian saints represented on mosaics and paintings in early chruches.

The composition of the Theseus mosaic is of particular interest. Unlike other mosaics with this subject, the hero is shown here in the very

Fig. 43. Theseus and the Minotaur.

centre of the picture. The hieratic arrangement of the scene produces the strange impression that the figures have been frozen in their attitudes. The whole scene, in spite of the drama inherent in the depicted episode, is deprived of the pathos and expression found in earlier representations. Theseus appears unconcerned with the outcome of the fight: his large eyes stare into space. We are now in Late Antiquity and the old myth seems to have changed its original meaning. It is no longer the duel itself that is important but the abstract triumph of the hero, who personifies transcendental virtues, over the evil represented by the Minotaur. The allegorical meaning of such a scene is clear, particularly when one considers it within the context of an official residence of the governor who represented the emperor, himself a sublime personification of all virtues. The stylistic qualities of the figures of both the first and the second period and the unusual iconographic richness set this mosaic apart as an exceptional creation. It also gives credit to the ability and the inventiveness of the artists active in Paphos at the time.

Poseidon Mosaic: Room 76 (Fig. 40).

High stylistic quality is also revealed by another figural mosaic found in Room 76 in the south-west corner of the villa. At present it is not accessible to visitors. Room 76 is square in plan with the rear wall forming a spacious semicircular apse.

Within a geometric frame composed of a double band of meanders with swastikas around a large field of interlace pattern, there is a figural representation. Unfortunately, the picture is now badly damaged. It was made of very small tesserae ranging from 10mm. (frame) to 2mm. (faces of the figures). Poseidon, god of the sea, with a trident in his left hand rides upon a sea monster through his marine kingdom. He is accompanied by his beautiful spouse Amphitrite, daughter of Oceanus. This motif was very popular in Antiquity, especially in the Roman period, and was often represented upon mosaic floors. Numerous representations have been found in North Africa as well as in Italy. The scene in the Villa of Theseus is the only one known from Cyprus.

Poseidon is shown as a strong, broad-shouldered man, half-naked except for the drapery partly covering his legs. Thick curly hair and a rich beard surround his head which is adorned with a blue nimbus, a mark of his supreme, divine status. He affectionately embraces his wife, holding her from behind by her left arm. Amphitrite, naked except for the mantle over her hips, is seated in three-quarter view to the right. Both her arms, with golden bracelets adorning the wrists, are bent at the elbows and slightly raised. With an unusual gesture of intimacy she holds Poseidon by the beard with her right hand. Her delicate and fine face is turned towards her companion. The curls of her long, brown hair descend onto her shoulders. Above the divine couple, there fly two small Erotes stretching between them a long banner blowing in the wind.

The carefree and graceful representation of the sea-ride of the gods may suggest the informal nature of the social gatherings which took place in the room. The style as well as some iconographic details, such as the halo around Poseidon's head, point to a rather late date for this work. Archaeological evidence, including coins of the second half of the 4th century A.D., indicate that the mosaic had been made in the later part of the century, possibly at the time of the restoration of the Theseus mosaic.

Achilles Mosaic: Rooms 39-40 (Fig. 44).

The main *aula* of the palace (nos 39-40) is to be found in the middle of the south wing and it is probably there that the Imperial governor officiated. The room can be reached by following the modern walkway to its end. It is divided into two parts; the lower (no. 40) faces the south portico from which it was entered through three doors − a large centre door and two narrower side ones. It is rectangular in plan measuring 10.60 x 9.30m. The apsidal

Fig. 44. The first bath of Achilles.

rear (no. 39) was slightly elevated in relation to the front part. Two steps revetted with marble led up to it. Marble revetment was also used for the floor and the lower sections of the walls, while the upper parts were decorated with murals.

The entire floor of Room 40 was decorated with mosaics. An aperture near the lower step, partly covered with a marble slab inserted into the mosaic, gave access into a huge underground cistern which collected water used for cleaning the pavement. The mosaic was composed of a wide Π-shaped geometric frame which enclosed a central field with figural panels. The outer band of the frame was made of a row of dark lozenges set upon a light background. The tesserae, all of local stones, measure from 12 to 20mm. The remaining part of the frame was composed of rows of simple meanders with swastikas and an undulating ribbon. At both ends of the frame there were two big squares containing smaller squares and lozenges. Each square contained an ornament called Solomon's Knot. The central square was filled with an interlace pattern.

In between the geometric frame and the figural panels there runs a frieze depicting scenes from a hunt. Clumsy Erotes, with or without wings, hunt wild beasts such as leopards, lions and bears. Armed with swords, the small hunters prepare themselves to confront the animals. They are dressed in *chlamydes* and ankle-high hunting sandals. The hunt takes place in a rocky landscape. Each of the figures is framed by an olive tree. The whole frieze is thus divided into segments which, nonetheless, form a harmonious unit.

The centre of the pavement was once occupied by four rectangular panels with figural representations. Each one was framed by an overlapping lyre pattern (elaborate guilloche). Only one panel is preserved in its entirety, but a few fragments of two others have also survived. They permit the reconstruction of the original arrangement and orientation of the pictures, each facing a different side of the room. The well-preserved panel represents the first bath of the newly born Achilles (Fig. 44). Although very little remains of the three other scenes, it is more than probable that they also represented different episodes from the Achilles myth. He was a beloved hero of Late Antiquity and scenes from the cycle of his life and his deeds during the Trojan War were popular in reliefs, murals and mosaics.

Achilles was the son of Peleus, king of the Myrmidones in Phthia, and of Thetis, one of the Nereids, daughter of Nereus, god of the waters. The immortal mother tried to ensure immortality for her mortal son. For this reason she held Achilles in fire and dipped him in the waters of the river Styx which had the miraculous qualities of protecting the body from all wounds. When bathing the baby she held him by his heel which thus remained vulnerable. A wound received at that spot during the Trojan War caused the premature death of the hero. The representation on the mosaic shows Thetis' first endeavours according to a slightly different version of the myth.

On the left of the picture the baby Achilles is seated in the lap of a somewhat robust nurse, Anatrophe. His eyes stare emptily at the spectator. Anatrophe, depicted in three-quarter view, her dull face in frontal view, is dressed in a long tunic with a mantle covering her lap. She is preparing to dip Achilles in the water held in a large cylindrical basin standing near the couch upon which Thetis reclines on a thick mattress. By the foot of the couch there is a column, and another one is visible in the background. Behind them hangs a grey-white curtain indicating that the scene is taking place in a palace. Depicted next to the nurse is a woman called Ambrosia bringing water in a golden jar. Peleus, the king, is seated on a throne on the other side of the couch facing his wife. He is dressed in a white tunic and a thick mantle. A white fillet surrounds his head indicating his royal status. In his left hand he holds a staff (sceptre). Behind Peleus' throne stand the three Fates — Clotho, Lachesis and Atropos — all dressed in a similar way. They have long tunics with mantles wrapped around their heads like shawls. Clotho holds a spindle and distaff, Lachesis a diptych, and Atropos is represented with an open scroll upon which Achilles' life was inscribed.

Iconoghraphically, the pavement is of great interest. The first bath of a newly born hero or god is a theme commonly found in Roman art, for example in depictions of the life of Dionysos or Alexander the Great. It is, however, on the mosaic in the Villa of Theseus that this simple act of the first bath of a newly born child acquires a more profound and symbolic significance, connecting the myth of Achilles to the vain human efforts to gain immortality. This representation sets the pattern for later depictions of the Nativity and the first bath of Jesus Christ as depicted in mosaics and murals of Byzantine and Mediaeval churches. Artistically speaking, the picture is not very successful. The plastic rendering of the figures is far from satisfactory. They are flat. The artist visibly failed in the manner in which he used colour to create the impression of volume. The foreground and the background of the composition are not well differentiated. The first row of figures appears stuck to the figures behind with no intervening space. The whole scene is essentially static, solemn, almost hieratic. It differs profoundly in spirit, style and composition from all the other pavements in the villa. We are presented here with a product of different times. The Achilles mosaic appears to have been made in the course of the 5th century A.D. and is the latest of all the figural representations from the villa.

W.A.D.

THE HOUSE OF AION

The Building and its Discovery (Fig. 40).

Excavations carried out in the autumn of 1983 by the Polish Archaeological Mission along an ancient street in front of the entrance hall (Room 69) of the Villa of Theseus, brought to light a pile of architectural elements. The way in which they had fallen onto the street indicated that they belonged to the wall of a house facing the villa on the north-east. The house has now been partly excavated and has received the name of **Aion** after the god who is represented in the middle of the mosaic found in the main room. The fallen wall has now been restored to its original position. It has in its centre a semicircular niche for a statue, with a half-column on either side and a cornice above. Of the house itself only three rooms have been uncovered completely (Rooms A-C), thus the full plan is not yet known (Fig. 40). The largest of these rooms (9 x 7.6m.) appears to be a reception hall (Room A). Its floor was decorated with figural panels enclosed within a geometric frame. Two smaller rooms adjoining the main hall on the north (Room B) and east (Room C) had geometric mosaics. The eastern room was probably a sort of vestibule, opening onto the reception hall by means of a tripartite entrance; on the south it communicated with a street leading from the harbour to the palace, while on the north a large door gave access to the inner part of the house.

The Mosaics (Figs 45-51).

The mosaic decoration of the reception hall (Room A) is composed of five figural panels within a Π-shaped geometric frame opening in the direction of the entrance (Fig. 45). The frame itself was made up of several borders, the outermost having the form of a band of white *reticulatum* ornament (rows of lozenges) upon a greyish background. Within this border there is a large square composed of a wave-crest and a multi-coloured guilloche. At the front, facing the entrance, there is a band of antithetical peltae, and in the front corners of the mosaic there are two squares composed of still smaller squares divided by rows of lozenges and inscribed with interlace. The figural panels were additionally provided with narrow frames composed of a crowstep ornament and a two-strand guilloche.

The pictures were set in three rows: 2-1-2 (Fig. 45). The smaller panels measure 1.99 x 1.31m., the large one 3.90 x 1.29m. All were made of stone tesserae not exceeding 2-5mm. in size. The mosaic is of exceptionally fine workmanship, the stones presenting a great variety of hues masterly used to render the volume of the figures and their individual character. All the pictures illustrate mythological subjects. At first glance they seem to be, with the exception of two, unrelated to one another and chosen in a haphazard fashion. We shall begin our description with the uppermost row of pictures.

The scene at top right (Fig. 46) represents the moment at which baby Dionysos, seated in the lap of Hermes, is about to be handed over to Tropheus, his future tutor, and to the nymphs of Mount Nysa. Three of them are preparing his bath, while Nysa herself and a nurse, Anatrophe, sit nearby. Dionysos is naked. A golden fillet and a wreath of green leaves decorate his hair and a silvery-bluish nimbus adorns his head. Hermes is shown seated in a dignified pose resembling an emperor on a throne, clad in an ankle-length purple-red mantle. Winglets at his forehead and feet facilitate his identification which is further corroborated by an inscription giving his name. All the other figures are also identified by names written in Greek characters. The young god is accompanied by three personifications: Theogonia, the birth of gods; Nectar and Ambrosia, the divine foods assuring immortality. The nymphs in long colourful dresses, have green wreaths upon their heads which enhance the dionysiac atmosphere of the scene. Two of them wear either bracelets, armlets or a

necklace. Nysa, their senior, has a broad golden diadem in addition to the wreath. Tropheus, the teacher, is dressed in a short tunic and trousers and has the pointed ears of a silenus and a wreath of green leaves with yellowish-red flowers upon his balding head. All the participants except for one nymph look attentively at Dionysos.

At first glance one is inclined to say that the scene is one of many such representations showing Hermes, who upon Zeus' order, rescues baby Dionysos after the premature death of his mother Semele and delivers him to the nymphs. Such scenes appear in Greek vase painting in the 5th century B.C. and later, on all sorts of monuments of Greek and Roman, as well as Etruscan and Coptic art. However, the unusual personifications accompanying the young god and the respectful way in which the divine child is being held by Hermes, his hands wrapped in drapery, indicate that this picture is not just a usual mythological representation of an episode from Dionysos' childhood.

The top left panel (Fig. 47) shows Leda, the young and beautiful queen of Sparta, wife of Tyndareos, who, in the company of Lacedaemonian girls, is about to take a bath in the Eurotas river. She is being approached by Zeus disguised as a swan. We are told by ancient mythographers that this liaison resulted in the birth of the twins Castor and Pollux and of Helena, the most beautiful of all women. Personifications of Eurotas and of Lacedaemonia accompany the scene. On the left side of the picture, behind an altar, stands a male figure. He is most probably a satyr wearing a panther's skin upon his shoulder and a wreath of long green leaves upon his head (destroyed). He holds an object reminiscent of a

Fig. 45. Mosaic floor in reception hall of the House of Aion.

pedum (shepherd's crook) or a double flute. This figure adds a dionysiac connotation to the scene.

The central and largest of all panels is composed of two scenes, one taking place on land (Fig. 48), the other on the sea (Fig. 49). Together they illustrate a beauty contest between Cassiopeia and the Nereids, daughters of Nereus, god of the waters. According to some ancient sources, Cassiopeia, famous for her beauty, was the wife of Cepheus, ruler of Ethiopia, and mother of Andromeda. According to other mythographers she was the beautiful wife of Phoenix (the eponym of Phoenicia), king of Sidon or Tyre. On our mosaic she is seemingly the Cassiopeia of the latter version. The victorious queen shown in the attitude of Aphrodite Anadyomene, reveals her fine body for the beholders to judge. She is being

Fig. 46.

Fig. 47.

Fig. 48.

Fig. 49.

Fig. 50.

Fig. 51.

crowned by a winged goddess, who, although she looks like Nike, a victory, is identified by a fragmentary inscription as Krisis, a personification of judgement. Aion, the judge of eternal time having no beginning and no end, sits in the middle. It is he who has given his name to the newly discovered house. He is the supreme and impartial judge of the competition. A nimbus surrounds his head of greyish hair adorned with a wreath of golden leaves. In his left hand he holds a golden sceptre, his right hand (only the fingers have been preserved) points towards the winner, Cassiopeia. A young boy whom an inscription idendifies as Kairos, a personification of an opportune moment, hands Cassiopeia a lucky lot just drawn from a golden vessel. From behind some clouds far above the heads of the participants, Helios, god of the sun, and probably Selene, goddess of the moon (completely destroyed), greet Cassiopeia from the heavens.

The scene on the sea (Fig. 49) depicts the three most beautiful of Nereus' fifty daughters: Thetis, Doris and Galatea. Beautiful and elegant in their dresses fluttering in the wind but angry and dissatisfied with the result of the competition, they ride away on the back of a friendly sea centaur Bythos, a personification of the depths of the sea, and a young triton Pontos, the surface of the sea. Bythos has crab pincers growing from his forehead while Pontos holds a rudder in his hand. A sad Eros riding a bull accompanies the Nereids. Zeus and Athena watch from above, greeting Cassiopeia with their outstretched hands. Representations of this particular story are extremely rare. At present only two similar but not identical pictures are known to exist, both on mosaics from Syria. Neither surpasses the Paphian example.

The bottom right panel (Fig. 50) illustrates the final moments of a well known musical contest between Marsyas the silenus, a virtuoso flute player, and Apollo, god of the arts, patron of the Muses and a remarkable player of the lyre. After the unsuccessful bid to win the contest, Marsyas was condemned to death by Apollo for daring to challenge the god. Apollo is seated upon a rock wearing the splendid attire of a *kitharodos* (kithara player), his head surrounded by a halo and adorned with a wreath of laurel leaves, embellished with a fillet of white and red beads. He is leaning upon his favourite instrument, the lyre, and his right hand, pointed at Marsyas, holds a golden plectrum used for plucking the strings. He is accompanied by a woman, identified by an inscription as Plane, who can be understood as a personification of the 'errant mind', that of Marsyas whose pride mislead him into provoking the god.

Two Scythians clad in Phrygian caps and short tunics execute the verdict. They lead Marsyas, who is dressed in a panther's skin, towards a tree where he will be flayed alive. Stricken by horror and grief, the silenus looks pleadingly at Apollo. Olympus, his young pupil, implores the god to be merciful. Marsyas' double flute rests on the ground by Apollo's feet. The scene is full of expression; the artist has managed to differentiate the psychological attitudes of the participants. Haughty and severe, the face of the god contrasts with those of the self-assured executioners.

The bottom left panel (Fig. 51) depicts a solemn procession of the young Dionysos through the world. The god rides upon a cart driven by a pair of centaurs with a lyre and flutes in their hands. A half-naked maenad solemnly leads the group carrying a quiver upon her shoulder. A small satyr, Skirtos, brings Dionysos fruits

— apples, pomegranates and grapes — arranged on a tray. Flowers spring from a square box. Tropheus, the tutor, mounted on a mule, and a girl carrying a basket on her head, follow the cart. A torchbearer once stood behind the centaurs; only his hand with a torch has been preserved. Of the god reclining on the cart, remain the crossed legs and a fragment of his blue cloak.

Although the dionysiac procession appears quite typical, its dignified appearance makes it quite different than that from the House of Dionysos in Paphos and especially those on Roman sarcophagi. There are no drunken satyrs or maenads dancing in ecstasy. All the participants proceed slowly as if taking part in a solemn religious ceremony, their faces are concentrated and full of respect for the god.

The unusually rich compositions in the House of Aion and the presence of unique personifications suggest that a deeper meaning underlies these pictures. One may suspect that all five scenes shared a common programme, the aim of which was to express a well defined message. The representations are tied together by the first and last panels, both having dionysiac themes. The first panel proclaims the good news of the Epiphany of Dionysos, a new supreme god, the saviour. This is corroborated by the presence of such truly unique personifications as Theogonia and the divine foods assuring immortality. The new Dionysos has little to do with the popular version of Dionysos-Bacchus, god of wine. He has become virtuous, born to save the world, to introduce a new order. His triumph is depicted on the last panel. Wherever he goes, the earth bears fruits and flowers blossom. All people can share in his triumph provided they are in-

itiated into his secret knowledge. A basket carried by the girl behind the god's cart is of special significance: it contains objects which are revealed to initiates during the mysteries of the god. All the other pictures are subordinate to this message. The story of Leda most probably portrays an irrepressible play of the senses, the aim of which, however, is the fulfillment of the god's designs. The contest between Cassiopeia and the Nereids, who in Greek art personify the sea with its waves, symbolizes in a poetic manner the struggle of wild nature, identified with the untamed oceans and seas, with the divine cosmic order. Cassiopeia, herself changed into a constellation upon her death, represents the cosmic order; that explains why she is being greeted by all the gods. The musical contest between Apollo and Marsyas has the same meaning. The silenus with his wild flute music embodied for the ancient Greek philosphers (Plato for instance) the barbarous uncivilized world; Apollo, the Olympian god, with his noble-sounding lyre stands for the cosmic order, while the harmony of the strings of his instrument stand for the harmony of the celestial spheres.

Looking at all these representations one recalls the words of the late antique writer Macrobius who in his *Saturnalia* (Macr. *Sat.* I.18.5-6) wrote that Dionysos embodied the other gods in himself. Thus he is Helios and Apollo and the intelligence of the world which is called Jupiter (Zeus). This strange monotheistic idea is striking in its deeply pagan aspects. One recalls that such a philosophical climate must have conditioned Julian the Apostate, the Roman emperor who in the early second half of the 4th century A.D. tried to reintroduce pagan cults in an Empire where Christianity had already been proclaimed the official religion of the state. The pictures from Paphos seem to challenge Christianity on moral grounds. The mosaics were made around the middle of the 4th century A.D. and their creation must have been supported by powerful protectors from among the old pagan aristocracy, deeply cultured and attached to the traditional values and creeds of the ancient gods which they were attempting to reinstate. Apart from their deep philosophical and religious importance, the mosaics from the House of Aion can be regarded as some of the finest examples of the so-called 'beautiful style' which characterizes the Constantinian renaissance in the art of the first half of the 4th century A.D.

W.A.D.

BIBLIOGRAPHY

BALTY J.: "La mosaïque antique au Proche Orient", *Aufstieg und Niedergang der römischen Welt 11, 12.2* (1981), 347-429.

DASZEWSKI W.A.: "A preliminary report on the excavations of the Polish archaeological mission at Kato (Nea) Paphos in 1966 and 1967", *RDAC* 1968, 33-61.

: "Polish excavations at Kato (Nea) Paphos in 1968-1969", *RDAC* 1970, 112-141.

: "Polish excavations at Kato (Nea) Paphos in 1970 and 1971", *RDAC* 1972, 204-236.

: "A legionary gem from Nea Paphos", *RDAC* 1973, 202-211.

: "Les fouilles polonaises à Nea Paphos 1972-1975. Rapport préliminaire", *RDAC* 1976, 185-225.

: *La mosaïque de Thésée. Nea Paphos II,* Varzovie 1977.

: "Aphrodite Hoplismene from Nea Paphos", *RDAC* 1982, 195-201.

: "Fouilles polonaises à Kato Paphos. Chantier de Maloutena", *RDAC* 1984, 294-307.

: "Researches at Nea Paphos 1965-1984", *Archaeology in Cyprus 1960-1985,* Nicosia 1985, 277-291.

: *Dionysos der Erlöser, Griechische Mythen im spätantiken Cypern,* Mainz am Rhein 1985.

ΗΛΙΑΔΗΣ Γ.Σ.: *Η Οικία του Διόνυσου,* Πάφος 1984.

HAYES J.W.: "Early Roman wares from the House of Dionysos, Paphos", *Rei Cretariae Romanae Fautorum Acta,* XVII-XVIII, 96-102.

MICHAELIDES D.: "A New Orpheus Mosaic in Cyprus", *Acts of the International Archaeological Symposium, Cyprus between the Orient and the Occident,* Nicosia 1986, 473-489.

: *Cypriot Mosaics* (Picture Book 7), Department of Antiquities, Nicosia 1987.

NICOLAOU I. and MØRKHOLM O.: *A Ptolemaic Coin Hoard, Paphos vol. I,* Nicosia 1976.

NICOLAOU K.: "The mosaics at Kato Paphos. The House of Dionysos", *RDAC* 1963, 56-72.

: "The topography of Nea Paphos", *Mélanges offerts à K. Michalowski,* Varsovie 1966, 561-601.

: "Excavations at Nea Paphos. The House of Dionysos. Outline of the campaigns 1964-1965", *RDAC* 1967, 100-125.

: "A Roman Villa at Paphos", *Archaeology* 21 (1968), 48-53.

: "Some problems arising from the mosaics of Paphos", *Annales Archéologiques Arabes Syriennes,* XXI (1971), 143-146.

: "Oriental divinities represented on the clay sealings of Paphos", *Hommages à M.J. Vermaseren,* Leiden 1978, vol. II, 849-853.

: "Three New Mosaics at Paphos, Cyprus", *III Colloquio Internazionale sul Mosaico Antico,* Ravenna 1984, 219-225.

VERMEULE J.C.: *Greek and Roman Cyprus,* Boston 1976.

Abbreviations

RDAC   *Report of the Department of Antiquities, Cyprus.*